Wheels Around Stirlingshire

by

Robert Grieves

A publicity photograph taken for Alexander's in 1935, when P 253 (WG 3481) was new and lettered for service on the Glasgow–Stirling–Perth–Dundee–Aberdeen route. This was one of no less than 67 Alexander-bodied Leyland Tiger TS7s new in 1935. Alexander's famous 'Bluebird' logo was introduced in 1934, replacing the 'Royal Blue Coaches' slogan.

© Robert Grieves 2004
First published in the United Kingdom, 2004,
by Stenlake Publishing Ltd.
Telephone: 01290 551122
Printed by Cordfall Ltd., Glasgow, G21 2QA

ISBN 1 84033 304 9

Reo Speedwagon GD 4095 of 1926 was owned by Duncan Campbell of Aberfoyle, who ran from there to Stirling via Gargunnock, where this picture was taken on service. In 1929 Campbell sold the business to Walter Alexander, who was steadily widening his network and acquiring many smaller bus operators in the process. Later, Duncan Campbell served the route between Aberfoyle and Kinlochard. Reos were frequent imports from the USA and were normally distributed by the Glasgow agents Cameron & Campbell. As its name suggests, the 20-seater Speedwagon model was no slowcoach, and was a popular choice of chassis for many bus operators of that period. The initials REO were those of Ransom Eli Olds, builder of the Oldsmobile car (an example of which appears on the facing page) in Lansing, Michigan, and a pioneer of the American motor industry. The 1980s American soft-rock group REO Speedwagon took their name from the same source.

FOREWORD

The usual mix of yesterday's wheeled transport is featured in *Wheels Around Stirlingshire* as with the other books in the series. While the accent is on road transport, paddle steamers also claim a mention, since on its western extremity the county includes a section of the eastern side of Scotland's renowned Loch Lomond. The name Walter Alexander is still immediately associated with bus and coach transport despite having disappeared from its base in Camelon many moons ago, and appropriately is given prominence. Other well-known names in the county with transport connections also feature. Hopefully memories will be rekindled for many as they peruse these pages. My thanks must go to the many transport men and women who have assisted, often unwittingly, with facts, figures and photographs.

As was the case in other Scottish counties, Stirlingshire had a relatively small number of motor vehicles prior to the First World War. The local registration index mark was MS, which reached 9999 in 1930 when WG was introduced as the replacement. One of the first cars in the county is seen here, without any licence plate, showing it to have been photographed earlier than December 1903 when motor licensing was introduced. This was a curved dash Oldsmobile, built in Michigan, the world's first mass-produced car and a popular import. The owner of this example was Colonel Edward Alexander, seen here not at the wheel but the 'tiller' with his wife outside their home, the Red House in Pendreich Road, Bridge of Allan. The car was licensed MS 2 when this became mandatory. A 12 h.p. Benz owned by Henry Adolph Salvesen of Lathallan, Polmont, received the MS 1 licence plates.

3

Blair's four-in-hand coaches carried passengers participating in the 'Trossachs Tour' in each direction between the steamers at Inversnaid on Loch Lomond and Stronachlachar Pier on Loch Katrine. The coachmen traditionally wore splendid red coats and grey top hats and here two of the coaches are seen alongside Loch Arklet, between Loch Lomond and Loch Katrine. These were the last regular examples of this type of transport in Scotland, continuing in service until 1938 when they were replaced by motorcoaches.

A scene at Inversnaid Hotel in Edwardian days, with a four-in-hand coach and its complement of passengers from the Loch Lomond steamer about to set off up the initial steep climb past Garrison Farm towards Stronachlachar. The hotel dates from around 1820 and in 1900 became one of the first in Scotland to boast electricity, generated by hydro power using the Arklet Water. Adjacent to the hotel were stables for the horses, a smiddy and accommodation for the coaches. Today this can still be described as a coaching establishment as it caters mainly for passengers on motor coach tours based at the hotel, now owned by Lochs & Glens Holidays.

After the demise of the four-in-hand coaches in 1938, motorbuses took over the run from Inversnaid to Stronachlachar. This 1960s scene shows George Buchan's three buses delivering tour passengers from the Loch Lomond paddle steamer *Maid of the Loch* of 1953 to Loch Katrine's venerable steamer *Sir Walter Scott* (built at Denny's yard, Dumbarton, in 1899 and still sailing today), whose funnel is visible to the right. This second sailing would convey the day trippers to the Trossachs Pier, from where Alexander's buses would take them onwards to Stirling railway station and the final leg of their journey by train to Edinburgh or Glasgow. George Buchan, who owned Inversnaid Hotel at this period, operated Loch Lomond–Loch Katrine services with these two former Ribble Motor Services Leyland Tigers, which continued to run in Ribble's red and cream colours. BRN 859 was a Burlingham-bodied PS1 model of 1948, while RN 7765 was a 1936 TS7 model with Duple coachwork. The Commer minibus was TES 60, new in 1962.

The western boundary of Stirlingshire extends to the eastern shores of Loch Lomond, and accordingly permits inclusion of a scene of paddle wheels on Scotland's best known stretch of inland water. This Edwardian view at Inversnaid Pier shows the 1899 railway-owned paddle steamer *Princess May*. At this period no less than five paddle steamers sailed Loch Lomond. Having arrived from Ardlui at the head of the loch, she would then sail onwards to Balloch calling en route at Tarbet, Rowardennan, Luss and Balmaha. The last of the Loch Lomond steamers, *Maid of the Loch*, entered service in 1953 under British Railways' ownership, replacing the elderly *Princess* which was then broken up at Balloch. When this photograph was taken, *Princess May* would have boasted an attractive livery of light grey hull and a red funnel with black top. A winter service on the loch was operated from prior to the First World War, lasting until the 1932/3 season when it was withdrawn, mainly due to increased opposition from bus operators on both sides of the loch.

Larbert railway station, 1903. The train in view is probably about to depart for Grangemouth, calling en route at Camelon and Grahamston. This was a relatively frequent local service at that time and a busy one too, since it predated the introduction in 1905 of the local tramway service. The locomotive appears to be Caledonian Railway Connor 2-4-0 No. 30 dating from the 1880s. Larbert station was built in 1892 to replace the original Scottish Central Railway mid-nineteenth century building, and was reconstructed in 1976. Today only two tracks remain, whereas there are seven in this view. The signal cabin has also gone, but the Station Hotel in the left background is still in business.

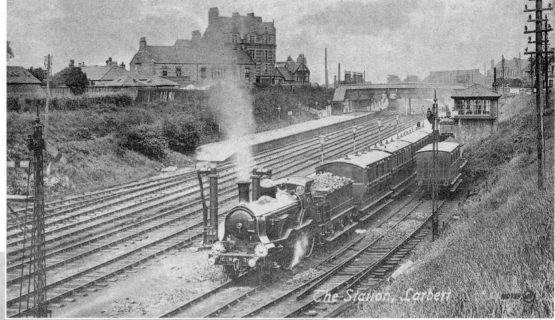

The Ochil Hills look down on the winter waters of the River Forth flowing below Alloa railway bridge on 27 January 1968. This was the final day of passenger rail operation over the bridge, and on that occasion Park Royal railbus M 79971 formed the 1230 service from Alloa. It is approaching the Stirlingshire side where it will stop first at Throsk and then Airth before terminating at Larbert. Certain journeys extended to Camelon, Grahamston and Grangemouth where the station closed on the same date as mentioned above. Freight traffic across the bridge continued briefly until 1 April 1968 when the line closed entirely. The tracks were later uplifted and the bridge itself dismantled and removed. (*W. A. C. Smith.*)

The next crossing downriver from Alloa railway bridge was the road bridge at Kincardine on Forth. This was the scene on opening day, 29 October 1936, and shows the first bus to cross the bridge, followed by a long line of cars and quite a few pedestrians enjoying the novelty of walking across. The honour went to Alexander's P 217 (WG 3450), a Leyland Tiger TS7 of 1935 which was bodied by Alexander and rebuilt by the firm to double-deck specification in 1943, becoming fleet No. R 340. Kincardine Bridge allowed Alexander's to re-route certain services between Glasgow and Fife, thus avoiding a detour via Stirling. The bus in this view had started its journey in Kirkcaldy and is approaching the Stirlingshire side of the Forth at Higgins Neuk en route to Larbert, Bonnybridge, Cumbernauld and Glasgow.

Falkirk & District Tramways Co. started operation in 1905, initially running a fleet of fifteen double-deck open-top electric cars which had been built at St Denis in France. The following year the well-known circular route was fully functional, encompassing Falkirk, Bainsford, Carron, Stenhousemuir, Larbert and Camelon. A branch line to Laurieston opened in 1909 but closed in 1924, twelve years before Falkirk's final tram ran in July 1936. Here car No. 11 on the circular service heads away from town along Graham's Road towards Bainsford. The attractive livery of the tram fleet was Prussian blue and cream, lined out with gold leaf.

Another of the F&D's original open-top cars crosses Bainsford Bridge over the Forth & Clyde Canal, again on the circular service. Note the silhouette of the conductor stretching to hold the trolley rope to prevent the pole jumping from the overhead wire, something that was liable to happen at this section. One of Falkirk's trams survives to this day. Single-decker No. 14 of 1931, similar to those illustrated on the facing page, was in use as a garden shed at Slamannan until 1979 when it was rescued and restored on behalf of Falkirk Museums. It now lies in storage at Grangemouth.

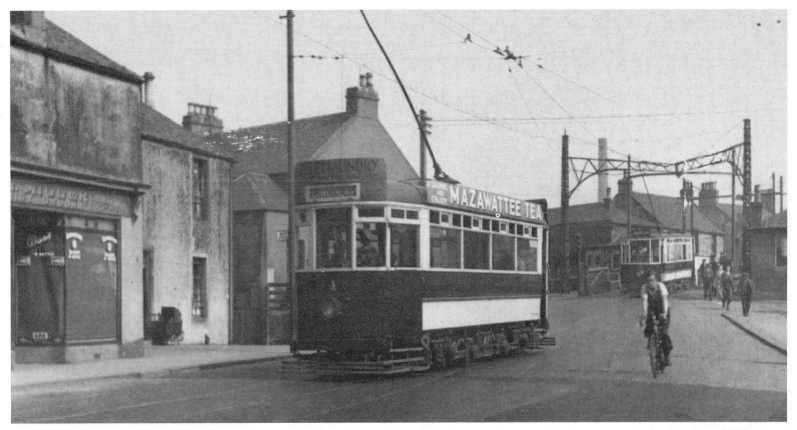

New single-decker 'pullman' cars built by Brush of Loughborough were delivered to the Falkirk fleet from 1929, and by 1931 a total of fourteen were in service. They gradually replaced the worn out double-deck trams, most of which were 25 years old by this time and quite decrepit. These new cars introduced a red and white livery, and moreover had the luxury of moquette-covered upholstered seats and saloon heating. This illustration shows Brush cars Nos. 1 and 6 on the Falkirk circular service, with car 6 crossing the canal bridge at Bainsford. The roof advert on car No. 1 extols the delights of Mazawattee Tea, a popular brand at that time. Although it sounded like it might have been the name of an Indian province, the name was a play on words for 'Ma's away to tea'. A further five single-deckers entered service in 1934 after purchase second-hand from the abandoned Dearne District Light Railways of Wombwell, near Barnsley, Yorkshire. However, these English–Electric cars only enjoyed a short Scottish existence, as Falkirk's tramway system closed in 1936. Stirlingshire boasted two tramways, the Falkirk & District Tramways Co. and the Stirling & Bridge of Allan Tramways Co. The latter commenced service in 1874 with horse cars, and although every other Scottish tramway advanced from the horse era to electric operation, Stirling enjoyed the doubtful distinction of being the only tramway town never to achieve this, although a single petrol car joined the horse-drawn fleet. The system served the route between Bridge of Allan, Causewayhead, Stirling and St Ninians until the last horse car ran in February 1920, with the sole petrol car lingering until May of that year when the company was acquired by the Scottish General Omnibus Co. of Larbert.

One of the earliest motor cars in the county was locally built in Stirlingshire by John Simpson of Whins of Milton, who is reputed to have constructed several vehicles. This 1903 example, registered MS 16, was a paraffin-burning steam car of 10 h.p. with dogcart style body painted dark green. It could seat three at a squeeze. In 1907 it was sold to a new owner in Harrogate, Yorkshire. Having initially trained with marine engineers Laird of Birkenhead, John Simpson became one of the founders of the Grampian Engineering & Motor Co. of Causewayhead in 1907. The Grampian works attempted to build both steam-driven and more conventional vehicles, but apparently without success, and it is doubtful whether any were produced commercially. Another early vehicle constructed in the county was the Larbert car, built by Major Robert Dobbie at the Dobbie–Forbes Larbert Ironworks, Foundry Loan, Larbert. This was a two-seater, 6 h.p. model and like the Simpson steam car was not deemed sufficiently reliable to justify further production, so was a one-off. It was registered MS 156 in May 1905 and ran as Major Dobbie's personal car for a few years. Unfortunately no photographs seem to have survived of this vehicle.

Another early car licensed in the county was MS 23, a 1903 Paisley-built Arrol Johnston with antiquated dogcart style bodywork incorporating seating for six. It is seen here in May 1905 being washed by chauffeur William Young after returning, incredibly, from a month's tour of France with its owner, William Gray Crum, a tenant of the Monro family of Auchenbowie, between Denny and St Ninian's, where this view was taken in the yard of the sixteenth century country house.

Striking oil in Stenhousemuir? Not quite. This was track repair work being carried out on the Falkirk & District Tramways' line near Larbert shortly after the system opened in 1905. Valuable assistance is being obtained from MS 121, a new Beeston Humber car owned by local engineer John Blackadder, who is seen at work with a drill driven by a flexible coupling attached to the rear axle under the watchful eye of two tramway company officials. Blackadder owned one of the original auto-repair and car hire businesses (established in the horse era in 1851) at Garrison Garage, Vicar Street, Falkirk, later known as the Blackadder Motor Co. Charabanc excursions were also operated. The Falkirk Tramways circular route, which linked Falkirk, Bainsford, Carron, Stenhousemuir, Larbert and Camelon, was unique in Scotland as it was the only line of four foot gauge apart from the Glasgow subway, which shared this unusual track width. (*NB Traction.*)

MS 317 was a 10–12 h.p. Wolseley–Siddeley four-seat tourer purchased by Archibald Strachan Barnwell of Bridge of Allan in May 1908. Scribbled on the back of the original photograph are the words 'Archie and his car at lunch time'. He has obviously been out for a spin in his new automobile, stopping for a break and looking quite relaxed, smoking his pipe and reading a book. 'Archie' was a member of the Barnwell family associated with the Grampian Engineering & Motor Co. of Causewayhead. The Barnwells were also involved with pioneer aviation. Archie's brothers Harold and Frank were both pilots, Harold becoming Vickers' chief test pilot. Frank visited the USA in 1905 where he met the Wright brothers, who made the first powered flight in 1903 at Kitty Hawk, North Carolina.

James Stewart's Victoria Garage in Dalderse Avenue, Falkirk, seen here about 1933, was a typical backstreet garage of the pre-war years. At the entrance on the left is the petrol pump, offering Pratt's (later Esso) fuel at 1*s*. 5½*d*. per gallon, while to the right is a selection of Pratt's motor oils. More interesting, perhaps, are the vehicles. Taking pride of place in front is a nearly new Coventry-built Rudge motorcycle registered in Stirlingshire in 1932 as WG 1239. The cars are (left) West Lothian registered SX 2844, a Fiat of 1929, and MS 6___, a 'Bullnose' Morris Oxford convertible of 1926, also locally registered in Stirlingshire.

During a Scottish Sporting Car Club event near Killearn in the late 1930s, driver Leslie Bisset got bogged down in his 1936 MG PA series car (YS 6491). Rescue was at hand, however, in the shape of a Fordson Iron Horse tractor whose registration plate – WG 8428 – was looped over the radiator filler cap. Embarrassing, perhaps, but at least it allowed Leslie, who was a regular competitor in such trials, to continue the contest.

Banner's Tontine Temperance Hotel, at the corner of Cotton Street and Buchanan Street (the main street) in Balfron, has been demolished since the 1950s. It originally sold alcohol and operated as a posting establishment with stables to the rear; customers could join the horse-drawn stage for Glasgow at the hotel. This scene from 1920 shows a variety of horse and motor vehicles offered for hire by the Tontine. Seated in the pony trap on the left is a young Alex Fraser, who later built and operated the garage in Buchanan Street owned by Shearer's today. Next is a carriage with Bob Shepherd at the reins, then a landau with top-hatted Tom Simpson in charge. SN 1369 is a left-hand drive model T Ford with Mr and Mrs Banner, proprietors of the Tontine, alongside, and John Fraser, father of Alex, at the wheel. John purchased this Ford from the Banners and started his own garage and hiring business. Partly visible behind is a small model T Ford lorry owned by the Banners, which at weekends was fitted with bench seats and used to provide transport from Balfron to connect with the Glasgow Corporation tram terminus at Killermont, allowing folk to visit the city before Rankin Bros. started their through bus service in 1922.

Rankin Bros. was a pioneer road transport company based initially in Chryston, Lanarkshire, shortly after the First World War, and which extended its territory to Stirlingshire in 1922 when a garage was built in the former cotton spinning village of Balfron. From this base in Dunmore Street (which passed to Alexander's and is still a depot for First Bus) Rankins' provided the first through services by motorbus to Glasgow and Stirling. By the mid-1920s the company was also pioneering publicity in the United States, with advertisements for extended coach tours to places as far afield as the Isle of Skye, John O' Groats, and in England to Devon and Cornwall. To venture by open charabancs to such destinations was quite an adventure 80 years ago, but Rankin's reliable reputation meant an expanding business for the company in this holiday market. The photograph shows three typical touring charabancs owned by Rankin Bros. in the mid-1920s period on an outing for local farmers and their families at the Buchanan Arms Hotel, Drymen. Leading is ES 3108, an Italian Lancia Lambda driven by Wattie Bauld of Balfron, followed by VA 2538, a French-built Berliet, and VA 2454, another Lancia. In 1929 Alexander's of Falkirk were widening their bus network and entered into fierce competition on the Glasgow–Balfron–Stirling route, pressurising Rankin Bros. to submit and sell out in April that year. Most of the better Rankin buses, such as their Albions and Leylands, became part of the Alexander fleet and continued to operate from the Balfron depot.

Callendar Riggs. Falkirk.

M. 104.

Around 1830 Mr Robert Barr started business in Falkirk cutting corks by hand and supplying them to aerated water manufacturers. However, in 1875 his son (also Robert) decided that it would be more profitable for Barr's to produce soft drinks themselves, which they did at Burnfoot brewery, Cockburn Street. Speedy success encouraged Barr's to open a factory in Glasgow's Parkhead district in 1887, and this Gallowgate site, now much expanded, is still the company's Glasgow base. Their best-known product – Irn Bru, or Iron Brew as it was formerly named – was introduced in 1901 and has certainly gone from strength to strength since. Today Barr's are the No. 1 independent soft drinks company in the UK. The Falkirk connection lasted over a century and a half until the long link with the town was severed with the closure of Barr's Portdownie premises at Tamfourhill. This picture shows Callendar Riggs in Falkirk in the late 1920s, when Barr's crate-laden horse-drawn delivery carts were a familiar sight (remaining so until the 1950s). Just visible is the back of MS 4964, a van owned by the old-established (1820) Headswood Laundry, which offered dyeing, cleaning and carpet-beating services. Also in the picture are two small Reo buses on the service to Laurieston and Grangemouth, including MS 8781 owned by Shields of Laurieston, who originally operated horse-drawn buses and sold out to Alexander's in 1930.

At 19.6 hands high (6½ feet at the shoulder), Barr's most famous horse, Carnera, was reputed to be the tallest in the world, named after Primo Carnera, an Italian heavyweight boxer. He was a familiar and much-admired equine figure in the streets of Falkirk, and is pictured here with John Corson, Barr's stableman, who was himself six feet three inches tall. Carnera died in harness while delivering drinks in Cow Wynd one frosty morning in 1937. He slipped, fell, could not rise to his feet again and sadly had to be shot by a local vet. Barr's final horse-drawn deliveries took place in 1952 when motor lorries took over.

The Falkirk & District Tramways Company diversified into motorbus operation in 1913 when two Commer charabancs were purchased. One proved unsatisfactory and was soon returned to Commercial Cars at Luton, but a further example arrived in 1914. This photograph was taken on an early private hire and shows LN 9772, No. 1 (on the right) with David Millar at the wheel, while No. 2, driven by John Chalmers, was MS 1176. This was commandeered by the War Department for war service in 1914 and did not return. Both busmen were trained to drive these charabancs, but had originally been tram drivers with the F&D (close inspection of the photograph shows each driver wearing their former tramway uniform caps with 'motorman' on the badge, soon to replaced by badges simply stating 'driver'). Davie Millar's son Willie also worked with the company, although on the engineering side, eventually retiring in the 1970s as Alexander's vehicle dock shop foreman at Camelon. John Chalmers was 'on the buses' throughout his working life, and was also later an Alexander employee, becoming one of the most senior drivers based at their Larbert Road depot, which had originally been the tramway sheds.

In 1919 a subsidiary of Falkirk & District Tramways was formed called the Scottish General Omnibus Company Ltd. The tramway company's twelve motorbuses were transferred to the ownership of the SGOC, or the 'General' as it soon became known. Its open charabancs were finished in a grey livery and familiarly called the 'grey torpedo cars'. The General was eager to expand not only its service runs, but also the private hire and touring side of the business, and reproduced here is a photograph of one of these touring cars, with a happy group on the occasion of the first annual outing in May 1919 for employees of 'the car sheds', as the tramway depot at Carmuirs was known. The charabanc was No. 10 (MS 2021), which had been new in March 1919 to Falkirk & District Tramways. The chassis make of this vehicle was Tilling Stevens and many more of this petrol–electric type were to join the fleet in succeeding years. Bodywork in this instance was also built by Tilling.

During the 1920s the Scottish General Omnibus Co. and its predecessor, the Falkirk & District Tramways Co., favoured the Maidstone-built Tilling Stevens for their bus fleet, particularly in the first half of the decade. This mid-1920s view in the workshops at the Carmuirs depot in Larbert Road shows evidence of both tramway and bus repairs, since the premises were shared by both methods of traction. MS 4558, one of several Tilling Stevens delivered in 1923 (with bodywork by Cowieson of Glasgow), is seen minus its engine and surrounded by the maintenance team, all very busy at various tasks. The wheels in the foreground were perhaps to be fitted to the Falkirk tram just visible on the extreme right. When the SGOC extended its Falkirk

area bus operations to Stirling in 1919, it had no base there, so all the buses on the Bridge of Allan to Bannockburn service were initially garaged at Larbert Road, travelling back and forward to Stirling at the start and finish of their duties. Temporary garaging was then obtained at the old Royal Hotel stables, Bridge of Allan, until 1920 when a new bus depot was built in Forth Street, Stirling. This remained in use with Walter Alexander until closure in 1983, by which time the new Bannockburn depot had opened, which then operated the services formerly based at Stirling. Larbert Road (now Stirling Road) remains a bus garage to this day, now the depot and area headquarters of First Edinburgh. Another depot in the area had been opened by Alexander's at Newhouse Road, Grangemouth in 1951 but was closed by Midland in 1988.

The route between Bridge of Allan, Stirling and Bannockburn was the focus of much competition from bus operators, hastening the demise of the old horse trams which were eventually withdrawn in 1920. The horse tramway company itself operated a couple of Tilling Stevens motorbuses which passed to the Scottish General Omnibus Company. In addition, buses and charabancs owned by a variety of companies including the Scottish General Transport Co. (not to be confused with the SGOC), based at St Ninian's; Taylor of Bannockburn; Campbell of Bannockburn; and Wyles of Stirling all vied against the might of the SGOC. Robert Taylor (whose father had operated horse buses from Bannockburn to Stirling) died in 1920 and his business was continued by James Penman, another Bannockburn-based company. This scene from 1926 shows Bridge of Allan terminus in Henderson Street at the former Union Bank house, with MS 4243, one of Penman's Albions (bodied by Stewart of Wishaw) waiting departure time ahead of MS 4919, a Tilling Stevens of the SGOC. A lady on the pavement looks over her shoulder as MS 6590, a brand new AC car, passes by. Notice that the General bus, which was new in 1924, has the luxury of pneumatic tyres while Penman's 1923 Albion was on solids. The liveries of both companies were red and cream, that of the General being a darker red. In 1929 James Penman, whose appropriate fleet name was 'The Borestone', sold his business to the SGOC, which continued to operate it as a subsidiary company until acquisition by Alexander's in 1930. Inset is a 1921 advert for Penman's Garage.

Originally a miner living at Braefoot, Plean, Thomas Forsyth started a bus service from there to Stirling in 1919 with an Albion charabanc which could also be used as a lorry. In 1922 he acquired the business of James Campbell, Lochrigg, Bannockburn, who had served the routes to Stirling and Bridge of Allan, moving operations to Campbell's former premises. In addition to the bus service, Forsyth owned a stable of horses including black Belgians, which were used not only on his council cleansing contract for the Bannockburn and Whins of Milton area but also for local funerals, when they'd be suitably adorned with black plumes. Horse-drawn brakes, carriages and landaus were also available for hire. Among several Albions in Forsyth's fleet was MS 5051, seen here at Albion Motors' premises in Scotstoun prior to delivery and driven by Peter Lamont who was later employed in a similar capacity by Alexander's buses. It was a 24 h.p. model of 1924 with 20-seat bodywork by John Stewart of Wishaw, who also built an enclosed bus body which was demountable and therefore interchangeable with the open charabanc seen here. It could also be used as a lorry for haulage work when necessary. Somewhat surprisingly for 1924, this vehicle was fitted with solid tyres and not pneumatics. All the Bannockburn operations were given up in 1932 when the Forsyths moved into farming at Greenhill, Denny. However, in the 1950s Thomas Forsyth's son Robert founded Easterton Garage and Recovery Services in Stirling Road, Denny, which at that time was situated on the main north road (A80), and therefore in an ideal location for repair work (Aberdeen fish lorries were good customers). Still going strong today, the business now specialises mainly in crane hire.

W. MARSHALL & SONS

MOTOR SERVICE STATION

'Buses leave here for AIRDRIE *via* SLAMANNAN
'Buses leave here for BATHGATE *via* AVONBRIDGE

For Hire — High-Class Motor Cars.

W. MARSHALL & SONS, Funeral Undertakers

MOTOR SERVICE STATION, COW WYND, FALKIRK

'PHONE 602.

116

Falkirk's first proper bus station was built in 1928 by Wilson Marshall & Sons of Standburn, and used exclusively for their own services from the town 'up the braes' to Shieldhill, Avonbridge and Bathgate, and to Slamannan, Longriggend, Caldercruix and Airdrie. The 'Motor Service Station', as it was known, at the corner of Cow Wynd and St Crispin's Place, later became the local social security office. Today the building is occupied by kiltmakers Burnside Highland Dress. Wilson Marshall's 'Venture' bus service was sold to Alexander's in 1930 along with several of the company's mainly Thornycroft fleet in a bright red livery, three of which (MS 6027, MS 8421 and MS 8153) can be seen in this view. Although the bus station was in Cow Wynd, the garage was in the village of Standburn where Marshall also operated a taxi hire and undertaker's business. Wilson Marshall additionally owned one of the first purpose-built petrol filling stations in the county, situated at Longcroft on the main Glasgow to Stirling road.

Falkirk's other bus station was built at Callendar Riggs by Alexander's in 1935, and although different in layout is still used by First Bus today. Originally Alexander's had shared stances in Hope Street, Falkirk, along with other local bus operators. This picture shows the bus station shortly after opening with an assortment of Alexander's vehicles of that period. The single-deck Albion bound for Maddiston was D 146 (GE 4710) which had started life in 1929 with Liddell of Riddrie, while the double-deckers were second-hand from Wallasey Corporation, with the open-staircase example from Sheffield Corporation. Note also the summer uniforms of the bus crews, with the drivers wearing white-topped caps, while the conductress has a light-coloured linen dustcoat with blue collar and cuffs.

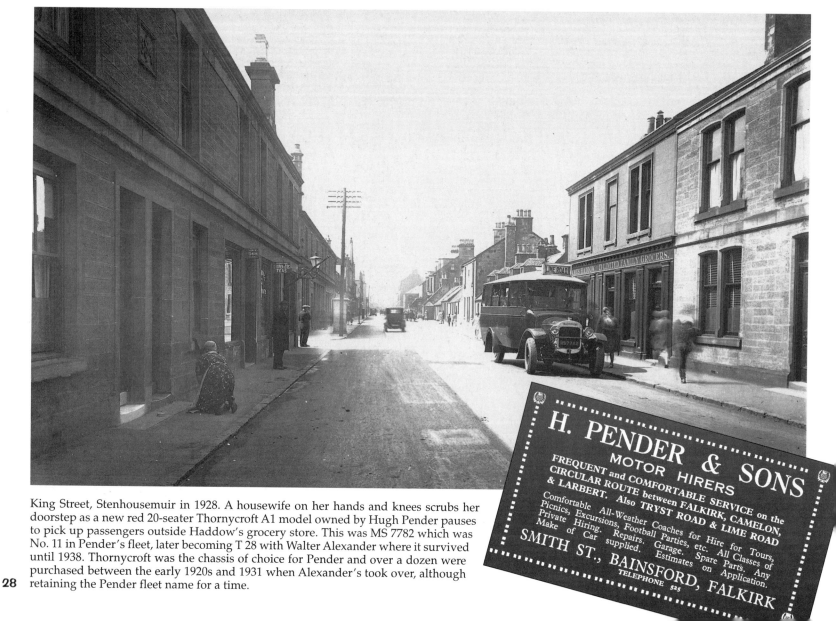

King Street, Stenhousemuir in 1928. A housewife on her hands and knees scrubs her doorstep as a new red 20-seater Thornycroft A1 model owned by Hugh Pender pauses to pick up passengers outside Haddow's grocery store. This was MS 7782 which was No. 11 in Pender's fleet, later becoming T 28 with Walter Alexander where it survived until 1938. Thornycroft was the chassis of choice for Pender and over a dozen were purchased between the early 1920s and 1931 when Alexander's took over, although retaining the Pender fleet name for a time.

Stenhousemuir in 1930 at the junction of King Street and Main Street, known as 'the point'. This scene is still recognisable today as the Plough Hotel remains at the same location, although much of the area is now pedestrianised with through traffic diverted to avoid the town centre. Falkirk & District tram No. 6 is seen on the circular service heading towards Larbert, and looking somewhat shabby towards the end of its life. Turning down King Street is MS 8270, an Alexander-bodied Albion of 1928 in the fleet of Hugh Pender of Bainsford, who operated in opposition to the trams around the Falkirk circular route. In 1931 Pender sold his business to Walter Alexander, whose fleet had itself become a subsidiary of the Edinburgh-based Scottish Motor Traction Co. in 1929.

MOTOR TOURING, 1924

ALEXANDER'S ROYAL BLUE COACHES.

LUXURIOUS COACHES FOR THE DISCRIMINATING PUBLIC.

Our Fleet of Cars for this Season's Touring consists of
Three 14-Seaters, Three 18-Seaters, and Six 28-Seaters.

COMFORT ADDS PLEASURE

TO A MOTOR TOUR,

the greater the comfort, the greater the pleasure.

There is not a more comfortable Coach in this District than our
28-Seater Leyland, on giant Pneumatics.

MAKE IT YOUR CHOICE AND RIDE ON CUSHIONS OF AIR.

SPECIAL NOTE.—All our Coaches are Brand-New 1924 Machines,
and are all Fitted with

PNEUMATIC TYRES.

For full particulars re Prices and Vacant Dates—Write, Phone, or **Call.**

WALTER ALEXANDER & SONS.

BROWN STREET (CAMELON), FALKIRK—Phone 266.

or

EDWARD STREET, KILSYTH—Phone 95.

Alexander of Falkirk is still a name instantly identifiable with public transport, despite no longer operating bus services. Walter Alexander started business in Main Street, Camelon in 1902 with a bicycle shop and general store, progressing in 1914 to own a solid-tyred Belhaven, built in Wishaw, which could serve either as an open charabanc or a lorry. A bus service between Falkirk and Bonnybridge was started, initially at weekends only, until a move was made in 1922 round the corner to the once familiar address at Brown Street, to premises able to house the growing fleet which expanded to cope with the operation of an ever-widening route network. In 1924, to accommodate the growing private hire and touring business, six new Leyland charabancs entered service (MS 4925–30). All are seen here, along with some of the bus fleet, about to depart on what was then Alexander's biggest charter to date. It involved fourteen vehicles which were used to convey Falkirk families to Major Monro's estate at Auchenbowie, between Dunipace and St Ninian's, for the Rechabite picnic. The bairns on the left are gazing wistfully across the tramlines in Carron Road at their departing pals, no doubt wishing that they too could share space in Mr Alexander's latest 'Royal Blue Coaches'. The inset advertisement appeared in the *Falkirk Herald* at the start of the 1924 season to proudly promote travel by the new vehicles, which were the first in the fleet to boast pneumatic tyres.

The old wooden bascule bridge spanning the Forth & Clyde Canal at Castlecary, photographed in 1927. Crossing cautiously in order to minimise the 'see-saw' effect caused by the passage of larger vehicles is one of Alexander's normal control (bonnet type) Albions, which were then the mainstay of the service bus fleet. At that period the company name was Alexander's Motor Service, which was painted along the broad cream band below window level. A large fleet number appeared amidships against the attractive royal blue livery. Castlecary was an intermediate stage on the route between Stirling and Glasgow, where the terminus was Cathedral Street, since the bus station was not opened at Killermont Street/Buchanan Street until 1934.

Walter Alexander's transport empire steadily expanded throughout the 1920s and 30s from his main base in Camelon. In 1929 the Scottish Motor Traction Co. of Edinburgh took an interest in Alexander's, and henceforth the Falkirk firm became operationally responsible for all SMT group services north-east of Glasgow, apart from the Dundee-based operations which did not pass to Alexander until 1950. The company's 1938 timetable listed depots in Aberdeen, Alloa, Anstruther, Arbroath, Balfron, Bannockburn, Braemar, Buckie, Cupar, Crieff, Dundee, Dunfermline, Elgin, Forfar, Fyvie, Huntly, Inverness, Kelty, Kilsyth, Larbert, Leven, Lochgelly, Macduff, Milngavie, Milton of Balgonie, Montrose, Newburgh, Perth, Stirling, Stepps and Stonehaven. As the bus fleet grew, so did the number of mobile maintenance and service vehicles. Typical of these was MS 8932, a 1929 Morris Commercial service van. This was based at Alexander's second depot, which had been built in Edward Street, Kilsyth in 1923 to relieve the pressure at Camelon. Seen with the van in Monieburgh Road, Kilsyth, is Henry Ferguson, whose brother Peter was also a mechanic at Kilsyth depot and whose sister was the office clerkess. At that time it was relatively common for entire families to be employed together by one company.

An atmospheric scene of light and shade in Henderson Street, Bridge of Allan, taken outside Elmwood looking towards Albert Place and the old bridge in 1936. These attractive Victorian buildings have since been largely replaced with new apartment blocks. The bus beyond the bikes is Alexander's P 66 (SO 3580), a Leyland Tiger TS2 acquired from the Scottish General (Northern) Omnibus Co. Ltd. of Elgin in 1931 and rebodied by Alexander in 1934. The Northern Co. was formed by Mullen & Thompson, who were originally based in Bannockburn in the mid-1920s, from where they operated the 'Comfort' bus service between Stirling and Glasgow. P 66 is passing through Bridge of Allan on Alexander's long route from Crieff to Edinburgh, which had a running time of three hours. This bus had been new in 1929 and was not withdrawn from service until 1953, when it was sold to Falkirk Football Club for further use as a shed.

The Scottish General Omnibus Co. of Larbert purchased its first double-deckers in 1928, a year before Walter Alexander did likewise. Both companies opted for new Leyland Titans, those for the General featuring Leyland bodywork with an open staircase to the upper deck, as opposed to the covered staircase on Alexander's orders. Seen here is one of the first four (MS 8456–9) prior to entering service. A further four arrived in 1929, all becoming part of the Alexander fleet when it assumed control of the General in 1930. When the first 'deckers appeared in Stirling in 1928, the local press printed an amusing nine-verse poem describing an imaginary conversation between McKenzie's 'wee' bus and one of the General's new Titans. This single verse probably typifies the reaction not only of the wee bus, but also of many Stirling citizens when first seeing a double-decker.

'Whit's yon?' The Wee Bus stood amazed,
And shook in every nut.
'A skyscraper on wheels it is,
Or I'm a silly mutt.'

vith the introduction of new services and
cies, the size of Alexander's fleet almost
ith the purchase of nearly 100 new vehicles.
e the company's first double-deckers (with
single London-type AEC bought in 1925)
nd Titans with Leyland's own bodywork.
ning extremely popular at this time with
hout Britain, and Alexander's bought eight
g several hundred more Leyland double-
llowing years. MS 9164 was originally No.
ut was renumbered R 1 in 1932 when the
ed a new system with a letter prefix which
ssis make and type of vehicle. The location
etween Denny and Dennyloanhead on the
ilasgow service, where these Titans operated
ency. The very tall telegraph poles were then
scene.

BARNTON STREET, AND POST OFFICE, STIRLING.

Barnton Street, Stirling, 1933. Sitting outside the post office is MS 8541, a 20-seat Bean which was delive
Service', which ran via the town from Riverside to Cambusbarron. About to overtake is Alexander's P 12
locally at their depot in Forth Street. This had previously been the garage for the Scottish General Omnib
until 1983 when the services based there were transferred to the replacement Bannockburn depot. Ear
operated a service from Stirling to Aberfoyle, as well as the mail bus to Thornhill and Port of Menteith.
Alexander's. One verse of a poem is reproduced on page 34, reflecting the thoughts of the 'wee' bus on se

In order to cop
increased frequ
doubled in 1929
Among those w
the exception of
which were Ley
These were bec
companies throu
in 1929, purcha
deckers over the
230 in the fleet,
company introd
designated the c
is Head of Muir
Dundee/Stirling
on an hourly free
a familiar roadsi

Alexander's expansion continued apace throughout the 1920s. This was a period when few families owned cars and railway fares tended to be higher than those by bus, providing a market eager for additional road services and tours. Alexander's made the most of the situation, building up a network of routes – mainly throughout central and eastern Scotland – partly achieved by a determined policy of buying out smaller competitors. In 1929 the powerful SMT (Scottish Motor Traction) Co. of Edinburgh acquired an interest in Alexander's, which led to much further expansion, in particular the major acquisition in 1930 of the Larbert-based Scottish General Omnibus Co. Ltd., along with Scottish General (Northern) in Elgin and the General Motor Carrying Co. of Kirkcaldy, immediately giving much wider geographic coverage extending as far north as Inverness. Among the new services launched in 1928 was an extension of the Glasgow–Stirling–Perth–Dundee route to Aberdeen, and this 1930 photograph depicts MS 8432 (later P 49), one of a large fleet of Leyland Tigers with Alexander's own bodywork, passing through the village of Causewayhead in the shadow of the Wallace Monument, while heading to Glasgow from the Granite City. Before the days of motorways, dual carriageways and bypasses, this was a long and time-consuming service and the 1930 timetable allowed seven hours, five minutes from Aberdeen to Glasgow (limited stop), while six hours, forty-five minutes was given between Aberdeen and Stirling on the regular service. Also reproduced is an advert from 1929 proudly announcing the acquisition of a fleet of coaches of the type illustrated.

Alexander's coachworks became a separate private company in 1948, at which time the firm was based in Drip Road, Raploch. The bus-operating side of the business had always maintained its own bodyshops within the central workshops at Brown Street, Camelon, where this photograph and the one opposite were taken in 1956. Shown here is AWG 353, a 1948 Alexander-bodied Leyland Titan PD1 (RA 15), which was based at Alloa depot. Alongside is Kilsyth-based R 384 (WG 3452) which started life in 1935 as P 219, a single-deck Leyland Tiger TS7, but was rebuilt as a double-decker with Titan TD4 specification.

Photographed in Alexander's single-deck body shop at Camelon in 1956 are P 554 (WG 8133), a 1939 Leyland Tiger TS8, and G 31 (AMS 561), a Guy Arab of 1946 which was operated by the associated company David Lawson of Kirkintilloch. Alexander's coachworks at Stirling had built the body on P 554, but that on the Guy was by Massey Bros. of Wigan. The head office and workshops of Alexander's, which had been on this site at Brown Street since the early 1920s, closed in 1987 when new owners Midland Scottish Omnibuses moved HQ to their depot at the former Falkirk & District Tramways premises at Carmuirs, Larbert Road (now Stirling Road).

Alexander's Stirling coachworks at Drip Road, Raploch, photographed in 1957, a year before closure since their new premises in Glasgow Road, Camelon, were to open in 1958. As may be seen, when orders were abundant the work spilled out into the street, due to space limitations within the factory. Visible in this view are Leyland Titan chassis (to the right) which were to receive double-deck bodies for Glasgow Corporation Transport. The Daimler CVG 6 chassis in the foreground was also to be bodied for Glasgow, becoming one of the large batch numbered D117–191. Behind this is a newly completed Guy Arab coach for Alexander's Bluebird fleet, followed by CWG 691, a Bedford O type lorry owned by the coachbuilders. Also visible is a new double-deck Leyland PD2/20 destined for Central SMT, in whose fleet it was one of the L557–566 batch (GM 8057–8066). The Drip Road premises had been Alexander's original Stirling bus garage, initially shared with another Stirling bus operator, Ferguson's Pioneer Services, who were acquired in 1929. When the Scottish General Omnibus Co. became part of Alexander's growing empire in 1930, the buses based at Raploch were moved to the former SGOC garage in Forth Street, thus allowing the vacated building to become the coachworks and in turn freeing up space at the original coachbuilding department in Brown Street, Camelon, which of course was also the head office address. *(Ian Maclean.)*

This 1947 view looks along Port Street, Stirling, and is busy with buses and bicycles. To the left, in Allan Park, is the garage of Rossleigh Ltd., one of the earliest and best-respected motor dealers in Scotland. Other garages in the town at this period included Westfield Autocar in Upper Craigs; A. France & Sons, Borestone Crescent; J. P. Jeffrey at Kildean filling station; Menzies Motors, Orchard Place; and Charles Sharpe, Barnton Street. The three Alexander buses were all Leyland Lion LT5B types, new in 1934 (P 288, 278 and 155; WG 2336, 2346, 2359) and all had 32-seat bodies built in the town at Alexander's coachworks. Stirling had been a coachbuilding town from the early nineteenth century. Since it was located on the old stagecoach route on the high road between Edinburgh and Perth, it was ideally situated for coach repairing and building. The oldest-established coachbuilder commenced business in 1802. This was William Croall of Shore Road, whose sons founded an even more successful coachbuilder's business in Edinburgh. Croall's partner was Henry Kinross, whose nephew William continued to develop and expand the company to build all types of horse-drawn vehicles, as well as railway carriages for the Scottish Central Railway which ran through Stirling. Another old-established Stirling coachbuilder was George Thomson of the Craigs and later Orchard Place. Thomson's carriages and coaches were even exported to Ireland, and also to the colonies in Victorian times. His fortunes ran almost parallel with those of Wm. Kinross, since both received contracts for railway carriages from the pioneer train operators, and both went on to build automobile bodywork when the age of the motor car dawned, although neither company remains in business today.

This Albion 30/45 h.p. three-axle four-ton lorry with caterpillar tracks was photographed at Drumtian Ford, which crosses the River Endrick near Killearn. Albion Motors of Scotstoun regularly used Stirlingshire's roads (and rivers!) to test new vehicles prior to delivery. Fintry to Lennoxtown via the Crow Road was a popular testing choice, as was the hill road from Drymen to Gartmore and Aberfoyle, both of which provided gradients and hazards equal to most which would be encountered in eventual working service. This view dates from 1928 and looks towards the Killearn bank of the Endrick. Today a pedestrian footbridge spans the river at this point.

The White Line Transport Co. was founded in Falkirk in 1928 by the Gibbs family. Their fleet of lorries was painted in a distinctive light blue and white livery and initially based in Thornhill Road, Falkirk, with the office in Stewart Road, before moving to Grangeburn Road, Grangemouth. A Birmingham base was also maintained to serve increasing business in the English Midlands. Apparently the name 'White Line' was based on the white safety centre line which was being introduced on roads throughout Britain at the time the company was established. Seen here is a Gardner 6LW-engined Albion model 59 10-ton long-wheelbase lorry, new in 1934. This was Albion's first heavy six-wheeler, although only about 60 were built. It was one of several of this make in the White Line fleet purchased through the Greenock Albion agent John Mitchell, who also constructed the bodywork, thus explaining the Greenock registration number VS 2509. Amongst the crates roped on top of the sheeted load are some which are stencilled 'Chemico nonclog lubricating oil', while others are marked 'Bovril'. Regular consignments of fish from Aberdeen were transported to the Glasgow fish market, while other contracts carried goods for the Carron Company, Grahamston Iron Company and Mains Cookers of Camelon. As was the fate of so many other haulage companies, White Line was nationalised in the late 1940s and the eight lorries and four trailers then in the fleet, including a recently purchased eight-wheel Atkinson, became part of British Road Services.

Stirling-based house furnishers Graham & Morton Ltd. were a well-respected firm of manufacturing cabinetmakers and upholsterers with their works at Burghmuir and furniture warehouses in King Street and Dumbarton Road. Their other main retail outlet in the county was at Vicar Street in Falkirk. Amongst their furniture delivery fleet was WG 7103, a 1938 Thornycroft Sturdy with Luton-style van body which would have been supplied through the Thornycroft Glasgow depot at Bishop Street, Anderston. Despite the long history of the company – which had been established as far back as 1830 – it failed to survive the onslaught of mass-produced furniture suppliers and business ended in the mid-1980s.

McCowan's Highland Toffee – the very name conjures up memories going back further perhaps than we would wish – memories of huge jaw-locking mouthfuls of delicious chewy sweetness, which came in wrappers featuring a shaggy Highland cow. Andrew McCowan founded the sticky business in Stenhousemuir in the early 1900s, opening his own sweet shop in Church Street, followed in 1924 by the factory which continues production today in Tryst Road. McCowan's became part of the huge Nestlé group for a period from 1959, but is now back under private ownership in the hands of the McCafferty family. In the 1950s and 60s McCowan's toffee was distributed in vans such as the Albion Claymore seen here. JMS 683 was new to the company in 1956 and its container type body was painted in an attractive livery of cream top panels divided by a dark green band from a biscuit- (or toffee!) coloured lower area.

A former Falkirk firm which favoured Albions for its transport fleet was Scottish Tar Distillers Ltd. of Lime Road, Tamfourhill. The company was formed in 1929 with the amalgamation of James Ross & Co. Ltd., Henry Ellison Ltd. and Gas Residuals Ltd. Seen here is No. 28 in their fleet, FMS 624, an Albion Clydesdale of 1954. Despite a major fire at the works in 1973, business continued until eventual closure in the 1980s.

Falkirk's best-known brewery was that of James Aitken in Newmarket Street, whose business spanned over two centuries from 1740 until 1967. One of several Albion delivery lorries in the fleet was this 3-ton model 463, new in 1935.

45

The Carron Company of Falkirk was founded to produce ironware – and particularly cannon – as far back as 1759, only thirteen years after the Battle of Culloden. In 1773 the company was incorporated by royal charter by King George III for its patriotic services; this charter was renewed by the Queen in 1963. During the battles of Trafalgar in 1805 and Waterloo in 1815, cannon were much in demand, and two examples which were used during the latter conflict have been preserved under the archway at the old main gatehouse to the Carron factory in Stenhouse Road. By the twentieth century, Carron had diversified from cannon to cookers and turned its attention to the manufacture of high-class kitchen and toilet fittings. The company lorry illustrated above, WG 2652, was almost a mobile advert for Carron's electric cookers, baths and ranges. Seen loading at the works, it was a 3-ton Albion model LHB 463 and supplied in 1934, one of several of this make in the fleet. Its bodywork, with hinged detachable sides, was built by Rogerson of Scotstoun, whose close proximity to the Albion factory made them a favourite choice for vehicle bodies. Note the use of straw to protect the enamelled surfaces of finished products from damage in transit.

DMS 907 was an Albion FT3 delivered to the Carron Company in 1951. The main product of the Carron Co. was initially the famous 'Carronade', a large-calibre cannon used by the military forces and navies of several countries in the eighteenth and nineteenth centuries. As the years progressed the company diversified into the manufacture of cast-iron drainage pipes, stoves, fireplaces and agricultural implements, and later a range of goods in plastic including sinks, washbasins and baths. Gas and electric cookers were also Carron specialities. A new firm, Carron Phoenix, now occupies part of the original site at Carron and produces similar items, but has no connection with the original Carron Co., which suffered liquidation in 1982.

'Smith for Service' was the familiar motto on the lorry cabs in the large fleet of Stirlingshire's best-known haulier, Smith of Maddiston. James Smith started business delivering coal in the early 1930s with a second-hand lorry, and along with sons James and Alexander built up the fleet to include new Bedfords and Leylands transporting, for instance, cookers to Aberdeen and fish to the Glasgow market. In 1947, when new vehicles were once more available following the Second World War, BMS 630, a rigid ERF, was introduced to the expanding company. Apart from home base at Manuelrigg, other depots were opened including Wigan, Willesden, Alloa, Glasgow, Stockton and Birmingham.